INSIDE PROFESSIONAL SOCCER

AFC AJAX

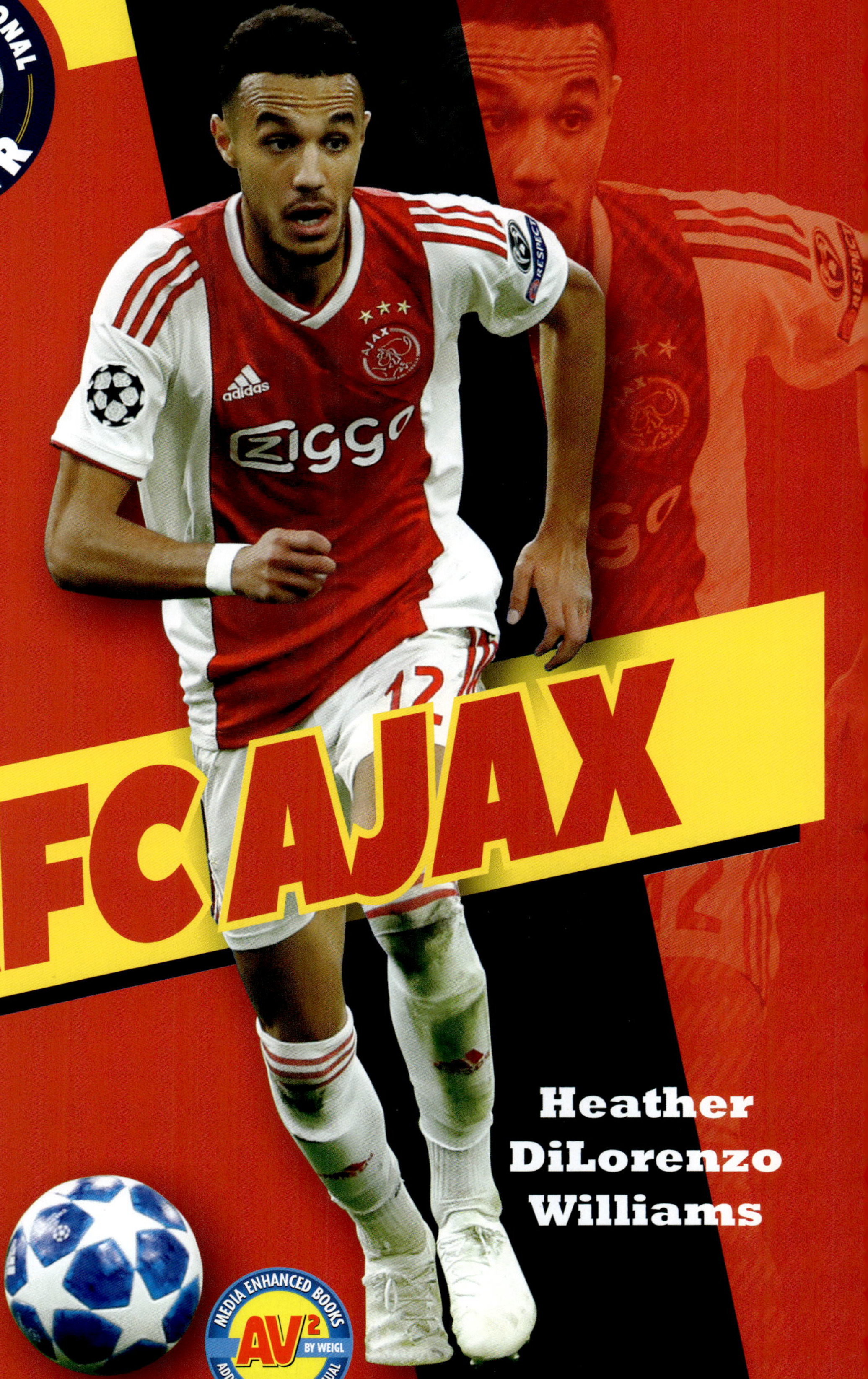

Heather DiLorenzo Williams

MEDIA ENHANCED BOOKS
AV2 BY WEIGL
ADDED VALUE • AUDIO VISUAL
www.av2books.com

Go to **www.av2books.com,** and enter this book's unique code.

BOOK CODE

AVM24548

AV² by Weigl brings you media enhanced books that support active learning.

AV² provides enriched content that supplements and complements this book. Weigl's AV² books strive to create inspired learning and engage young minds in a total learning experience.

Your AV² Media Enhanced books come alive with...

Audio
Listen to sections of the book read aloud.

Video
Watch informative video clips.

Embedded Weblinks
Gain additional information for research.

Try This!
Complete activities and hands-on experiments.

Key Words
Study vocabulary, and complete a matching word activity.

Quizzes
Test your knowledge.

Slide Show
View images and captions, and prepare a presentation.

... and much, much more!

Published by AV² by Weigl
350 5th Avenue, 59th Floor
New York, NY 10118
Website: www.av2books.com

Library of Congress Control Number: 2018968473

ISBN 978-1-7911-0595-2 (hardcover)
ISBN 978-1-7911-0596-9 (multi-user eBook)
ISBN 978-1-7911-0597-6 (single-user eBook)

Printed in Guangzhou, China
1 2 3 4 5 6 7 8 9 0 23 22 21 20 19

022019
102318

Project Coordinator: John Willis   Designer: Terry Paulhus

Every reasonable effort has been made to trace ownership and to obtain permission to reprint copyright material. The publishers would be pleased to have any errors or omissions brought to their attention so that they may be corrected in subsequent printings.

The publisher acknowledges Alamy, Getty Images, and iStock as its primary image suppliers for this title.

CONTENTS

Introduction

Amsterdam, a city in the Netherlands, is known for its bright colors and unique culture. It is also home to one of the world's most exciting soccer **clubs**, Amsterdamsche Football Club Ajax, or AFC Ajax. Soccer is called football in most European countries.

AFC Ajax is named after a legendary war hero from Greek mythology. The team is a reflection of its namesake. It is one of the most successful soccer teams of all time. Ajax introduced the world to a style of play called **total football**. This concept changed the way soccer teams around the world played the game. Ajax's youth academy has produced some of the greatest soccer players in the sport's history.

Ajax Amsterdam has a reputation for developing young players, such as Dani de Wit, into some of soccer's most sought-after stars.

Ajax has dominated the top division of Dutch football, the Eredivisie, for decades. Although it is not the world power it once was, its record number of trophies and awe-inspiring history make Ajax a team worth getting to know.

Daley Blind has played for Ajax for most of his life. He joined Ajax's youth team at age 8. Blind recently returned to Ajax after a few years in England.

AFC AJAX

Arena Johan Cruyff ArenA

Division Eredivisie

Head Coach Erik ten Hag

Location Amsterdam, Netherlands

FIFA Club World Cups 2

Nicknames *de Godenzonen* ("Sons of the Gods")

3 Home Stadiums

33 League Titles

19 Players with 100-plus Goals

70 Total Trophies

49,670 Average 2017–18 Home Attendance

History

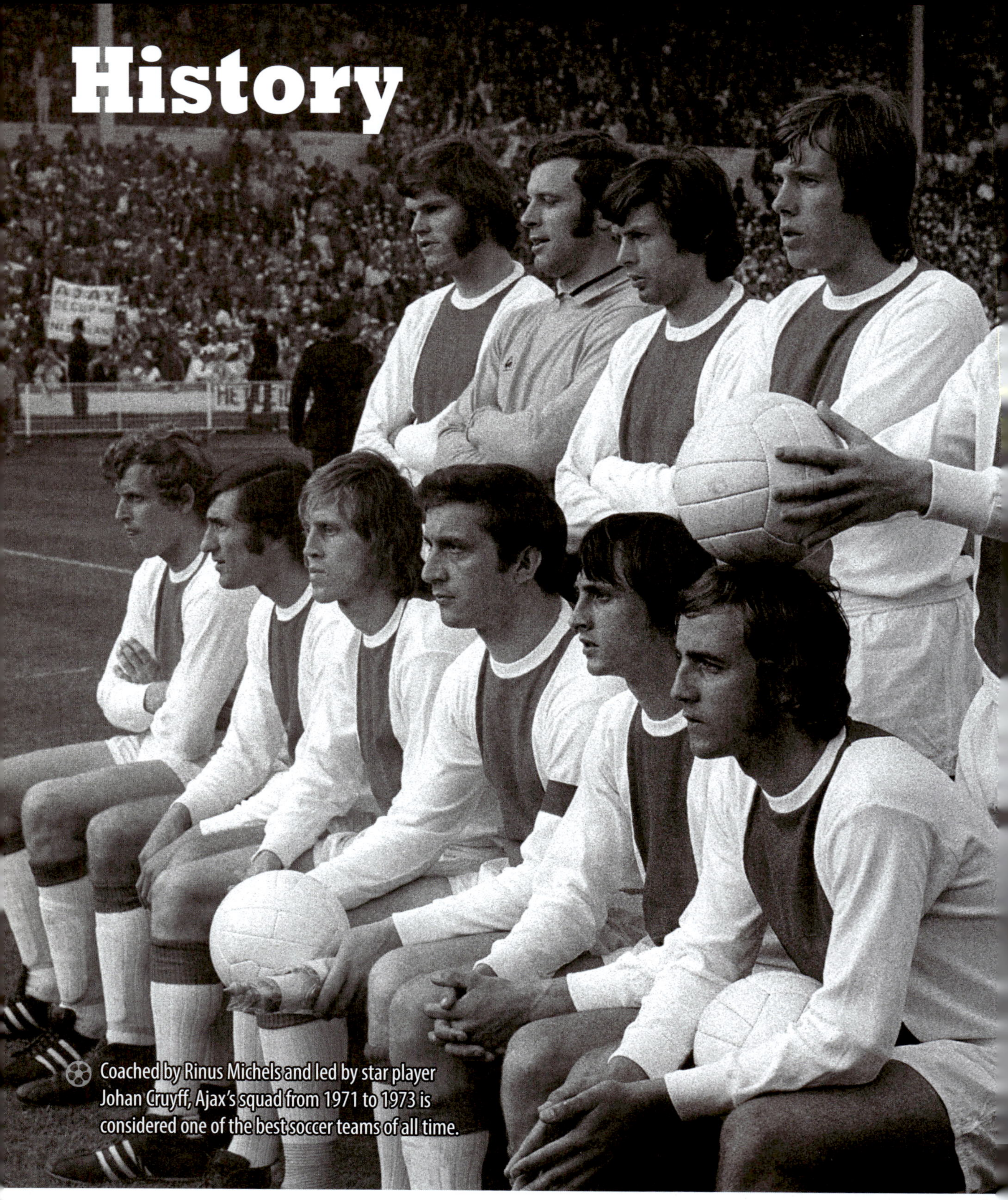

Coached by Rinus Michels and led by star player Johan Cruyff, Ajax's squad from 1971 to 1973 is considered one of the best soccer teams of all time.

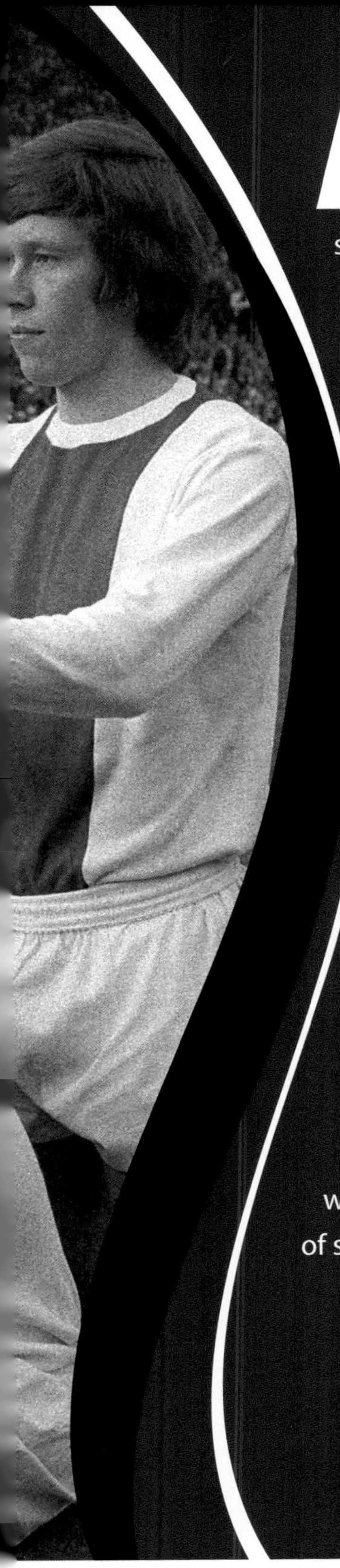

Ajax was founded in 1900 by three friends, Carel Reeser, Han Dade, and the team's first chairman, Floris Stempel. AFC Ajax struggled for the first 15 years, playing mostly in the second division of Dutch soccer. The arrival of legendary coach Jack Reynolds changed everything. He was appointed in 1915 and led Ajax to many years of success. Ajax would become well known for the unique methods Reynolds brought to the team. In 1918, Ajax won its first of many national titles. It dominated Dutch soccer in the 1920s and 1930s.

Ajax moved into De Meer Stadion in 1934. The team was both a founding member of the Eredivisie in 1956 and the first Eredivisie champion. It became the first team from the Netherlands to play in the European Cup Winners' Cup in 1961. Ajax went on to win the Winners' Cup in 1971 and the Intercontinental Cup in 1972. Ajax's 1971–72 season is considered one of the greatest seasons in the sport's history.

Throughout the next four decades, Ajax continued to win national, European, and world honors. Although it must often battle rivals Feyenoord and PSV Eindhoven for the Eredivisie's top spot, Ajax remains a powerhouse. There has rarely been a season since 1915 when the team did not win a trophy or play in some of soccer's top competitions.

Ajax captain Velibor Vasović led his team to its 1971 European Cup win.

The Arena

The Netherlands' **Queen Beatrix** officially opened the Johan Cruyff ArenA by pulling a cord that caused a giant floor-to-ceiling **curtain** surrounding the field to fall one section at a time.

Johan Cruyff ArenA was one of 12 stadiums chosen to host matches for the 2020 Union of European Football Associations (UEFA) European Football Championship.

During its first decade, Ajax played in open fields with no bleachers or locker rooms. The team's first real stadium was *Het Houten Stadion*, "Wooden Stadium." Ajax played there until 1934, when it moved to De Meer Stadion. De Meer was designed by a club member and commissioner and could hold 19,000 people. Bigger games were played at *Olympisch Stadion*, "Olympic Stadium," which had been built to host the 1928 Summer Olympics.

In 1996, state-of-the-art Amsterdam ArenA became the official home of Ajax. Renamed Johan Cruyff ArenA in 2018, the stadium seats nearly 54,000 people. It is the largest stadium in the Netherlands. Johan Cruyff ArenA has a retractable roof that takes 18 minutes to open or close. Special artificial lighting and underground irrigation maintain the natural grass turf.

Johan Cruyff ArenA began a three-phase renovation in 2017. The number of seats will not change, but more space will be added for walkways, restaurants, and restrooms. The stadium's improvements will be completed in time to host some of soccer's biggest competitions.

De Meer Stadion was home to Ajax for 62 years and remains an important part of the club's history.

Where They Play

Arena
Johan Cruyff ArenA

Location
Amsterdam, Netherlands

Broke Ground
1993

Completed
1996

Field Design
The stadium looks like a giant UFO, with its retractable roof covering a traditional grass soccer pitch with two fully covered tiers of seating.

Features
- Stairwells with diagonally linked round holes that look like soccer shoelaces.
- One of the steepest arenas in Europe, with the second tier of seating at a 37-degree angle.
- Ajax museum contains more than 100 years of team artifacts.

POLAND

2018–19 EREDIVISIE TEAMS

1 ADO Den Haag *(The Hague, Netherlands)*
★2 Ajax *(Amsterdam, Netherlands)*
3 AZ *(Alkmaar, Netherlands)*
4 Emmen *(Emmen, Netherlands)*
5 Excelsior *(Rotterdam, Netherlands)*
6 Feyenoord *(Rotterdam, Netherlands)*
7 Fortuna Sittard *(Sittard, Netherlands)*
8 de Graafschap *(Doetinchem, Netherlands)*
9 Groningen *(Groningen, Netherlands)*
10 Heerenveen *(Heerenveen, Netherlands)*
11 Heracles Almelo *(Almelo, Netherlands)*
12 NAC Breda *(Breda, Netherlands)*
13 PEC Zwolle *(Zwolle, Netherlands)*
14 PSV *(Eindhoven, Netherlands)*
15 Utrecht *(Utrecht, Netherlands)*
16 Vitesse *(Arnhem, Netherlands)*
17 VVV-Venlo *(Venlo, Netherlands)*
18 Willem II *(Tilburg, The Netherlands)*

The Uniforms

Dutch cable company Ziggo has been Ajax's main sponsor since 2015. Its logo is featured on all jerseys worn by Ajax players.

AFC Ajax's colors have always been the red, black, and white of the Amsterdam flag. The first official **kit** was introduced in 1910. It had a red and white striped jersey and black shorts. When Ajax began playing in the first division of Dutch soccer, it had to change its uniform because another team's was exactly the same. Ajax switched to white jerseys with a wide red stripe in the center and white shorts and socks with red trim. The home kit has not changed much from this design. Ajax wears black, gold, and white for away matches.

The Ajax logo has changed four times. In 1928, the club adopted a logo featuring the head of the Greek warrior Ajax. Today's logo is similar, but the hero is drawn with 11 lines to represent the 11 players on a soccer field. Today, players wear three stars above the logo. Each star represents 10 Eredivisie championships.

Before the club adopted the simple line drawing of the Greek hero Ajax in 1991, the logo included a much more detailed drawing of the figure, complete with a battle scene drawn on his helmet.

Goalie Gear

André Onana has a reputation for making impossible saves, especially on close-range shots and penalty kicks.

Goalkeepers must stand out from field players and officials. They usually wear long sleeves and colorful jerseys. Goalies can wear pants instead of shorts. Some goalkeeping uniforms are padded to protect from impact. Most goalies wear special goalkeeping gloves. These gloves have rubber surfaces to help grip the ball. Goalkeeper gloves often contain plastic spines to protect the goalie's hands from injuries.

The current goalkeeper for AFC Ajax is André Onana. He wears black, lime green, or turquoise in the Ajax goal. Onana is a product of FC Barcelona's La Masia youth academy. The 20-year-old may be one of soccer's upcoming goalkeeping stars. He plays a "sweeper-keeper" style, meaning he is skilled at handling the ball with his feet as well as stopping shots. Onana often comes out of the penalty box to play the ball into the field.

Ajax backup goalkeeper Kostas Lamprou left Greece at age 13 to join Ajax's youth academy. He played for Eredivisie rivals Feyenoord and Willem II before returning to Ajax as part of the senior squad.

The Coaches

Current Ajax head coach Erik ten Hag was an assistant coach to the legendary Pep Guardiola in Germany. Guardiola played at Barcelona for Ajax legend Johan Cruyff.

Erik ten Hag designs each training session based on every player's individual performance in their most recent game.

AFC Ajax has had 40 coaches in 118 years. Five men served as coach more than one time. The current coach is Erik ten Hag. He is known for observing each player's every move, behavior, and emotional reaction, then forming a strategy based on the exact personalities and strengths of these players.

JACK REYNOLDS Jack Reynolds was the man who transformed Ajax into a powerhouse. He was also the team's longest-serving coach. Reynolds was the head coach of Ajax from 1915 to 1925, 1928 to 1940, and 1945 to 1947. He was responsible for moving and keeping Ajax in the top tier of Dutch soccer permanently. Reynolds led the team to eight division championships and two national cups.

RINUS MICHELS Rinus Michels played for Ajax for 12 years before becoming coach in 1965. Michels learned the foundations of total football under Jack Reynolds. Michels is credited for formulating and introducing this style of play to the world. Michels won eight trophies with Ajax, including the team's first European Cup. He is considered the most influential tactician in the history of the sport.

LOUIS VAN GAAL One of Ajax's most successful coaches, Louis van Gaal won 11 titles, including the Intercontinental Cup. Under his leadership, Ajax became only the second club to have won all three major European club competitions. Van Gaal is known for being able to create a formation based on the team he had, rather than forcing his team into a set formation. Van Gaal coached at Ajax from 1991 to 1997.

Fans Around the World

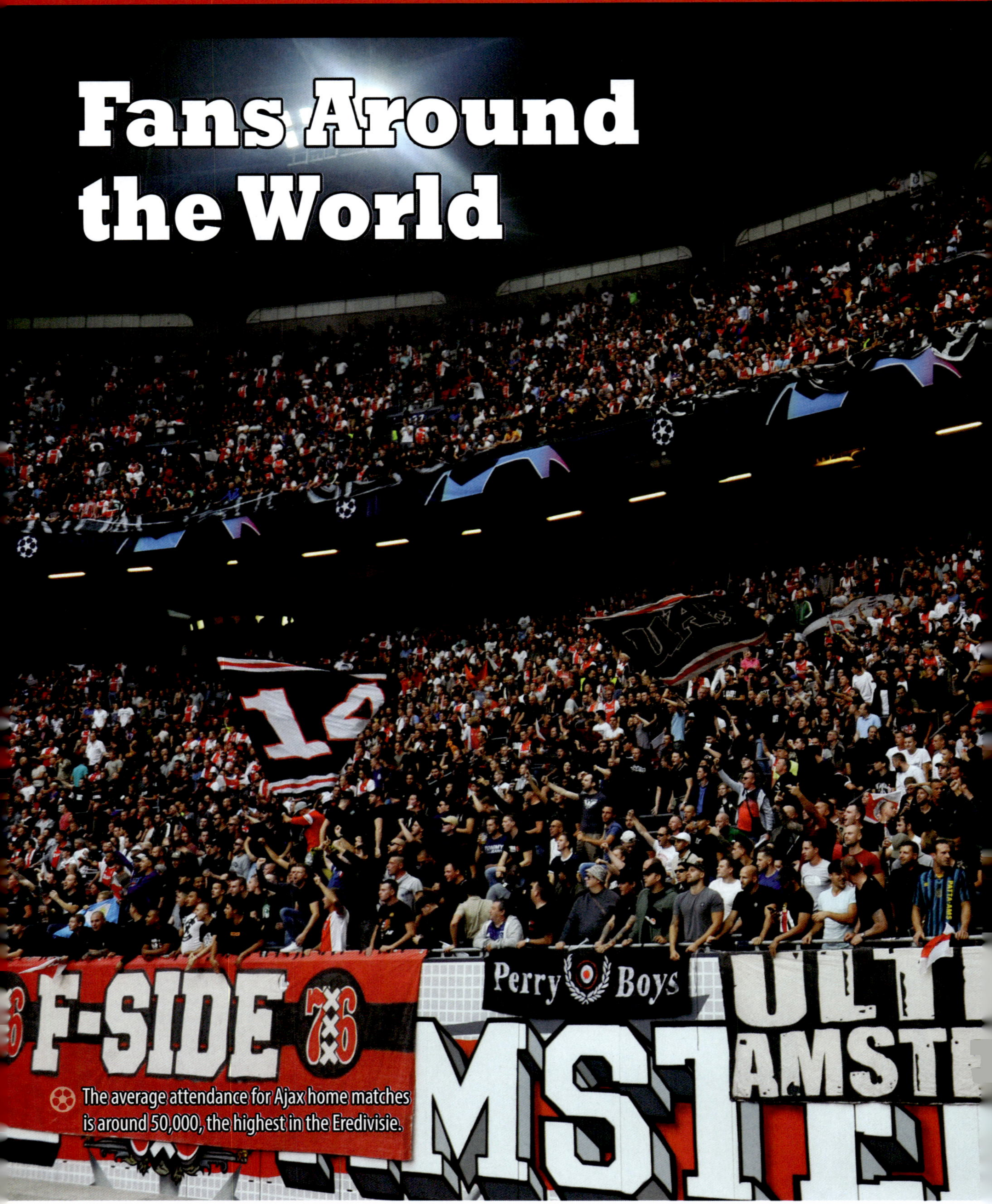

The average attendance for Ajax home matches is around 50,000, the highest in the Eredivisie.

Ajax is the most supported soccer team in the Netherlands. There are around 4 million Dutch Ajax fans, and the team's official supporters' club has more than 90,000 members. It is called the Supporters Club Ajax. Ajax has close to 100,000 Twitter followers and 2.5 million followers on Facebook. The two main **ultras** groups are F-Side and VAK410. Both groups are named for their designated seating areas during home matches.

Fans of Ajax are known for holding up sarcastic signs and banners during games. Ajax's biggest rival is Feyenoord, from Rotterdam. Ajax fans hold up many of these signs during "The Classic," a yearly game between the two teams. After big wins, fans often gather at the Ajax training ground and cheer during practice, much like they would at an actual game.

Fan Traditions

#1 Ultras gather under the bridge leading to the main entrance of the stadium and sing team songs, dance, and wave flares in a display known as *entrada*, "entry."

#2 A common chant during Ajax matches is sung to the tune of "You Are My Sunshine."

Legends of the Past

Many great players have suited up for AFC Ajax. A few of them have become icons of the team and the city it represents.

Marco van Basten

Marco van Basten is considered one of the best **forwards** in the history of professional soccer. Van Basten scored 142 goals for Ajax. He led the Eredivisie in scoring from 1984 to 1987 and scored the winning goal for Ajax in the 1987 UEFA Cup Winners' Cup Final. Van Basten was known for scoring dramatic, acrobatic goals, and for always finding a way to take a shot, even at awkward angles or through multiple **defenders**. He also sometimes scored with dramatic headers and bicycle kick shots. Van Basten played for the Dutch national team. A severe ankle injury ended his career at age 30 and he became a coach.

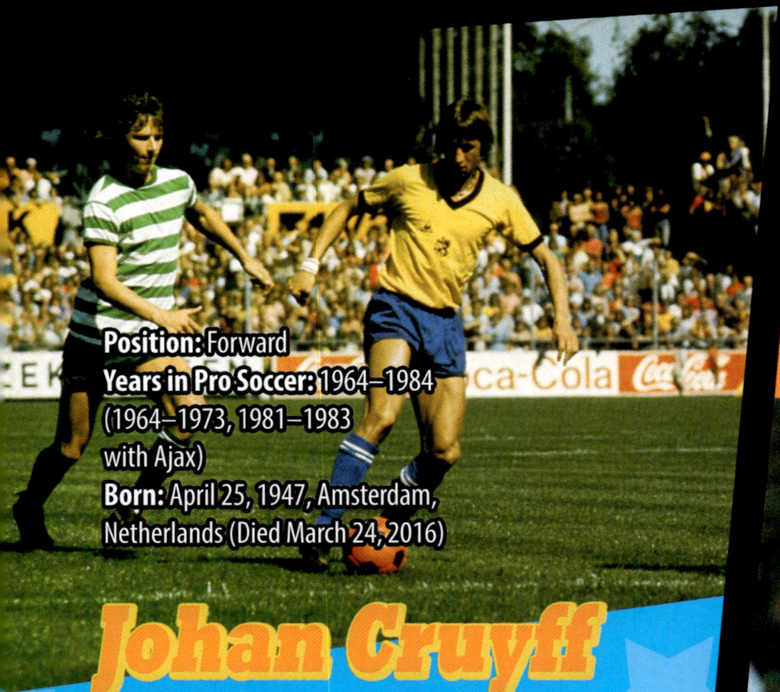

Position: Forward
Years in Pro Soccer: 1964–1984 (1964–1973, 1981–1983 with Ajax)
Born: April 25, 1947, Amsterdam, Netherlands (Died March 24, 2016)

Johan Cruyff

Johan Cruyff was one of the greatest soccer players of all time. Cruyff debuted for Ajax at age 17 and went on to lead the team to eight Eredivisie titles and three European championships. Cruyff holds the record for most goals scored for Ajax. He wore the number 14 for the first time by accident, but after winning that game, he superstitiously insisted on wearing it permanently. Ajax retired his number in 2007. A master of the total football concept on and off the field, he established Barcelona's youth training program during his time as coach there. Much like the Ajax Youth Academy, it produced some of the world's best players.

Position: Forward
Years in Pro Soccer: 1981–1995 (1982–1987 with Ajax)
Born: October 31, 1964 Utrecht, Netherlands

Dennis Bergkamp

Dennis Bergkamp joined the Ajax Youth Academy at age 11 and debuted for the pro team in 1986. He was the top scorer in the Eredivisie from 1991 to 1993 and helped Ajax return to a period of success in the early 1990s. Bergkamp scored 123 goals in 246 matches for Ajax. He is regarded as one of the best players of his generation. As part of the Netherlands national team, Bergkamp was second runner-up as Fédération Internationale de Football Association (FIFA) World Player of the Year twice, in 1993 and 1997. In 2004, soccer legend Pelé named him one of the greatest 100 living soccer players.

Position: Forward
Years in Pro Soccer: 1986–2006
(1986–1993 with Ajax)
Born: May 10, 1969, Amsterdam, Netherlands

Sjaak Swart

Midfielder Sjaak Swart is known as "Mr. Ajax." The son of a Jewish fisherman, his family hid during World War II and survived the extermination of 75 percent of the Jewish population of the Netherlands. Swart joined Ajax's youth academy team in 1949 and was named to the main team in 1956. He remained a consistent player despite Ajax's struggles in the 1960s. Swart, along with teammate Johan Cruyff, was part of Ajax's renowned 1972 team. He played more games for Ajax than any other player in the club's history. Swart also made 31 appearances for the Netherlands national team.

Position: Midfielder
Years in Pro Soccer: 1956–1973
(Entire career with Ajax)
Born: July 3, 1938
Muiderberg, Netherlands

Stars of Today

Today's AFC Ajax team is made up of many young, talented players who have proven that they are among the best in the league.

Kasper Dolberg

Kasper Dolberg joined Ajax in 2016 at age 18. He immediately became a scoring machine for the team. In his first year with Ajax, Dolberg scored 23 goals in 47 matches. He is the youngest non-Dutch player to score a **hat trick** for Ajax. Dolberg has speed and skill, and can score with either foot. Although he has been courted by larger clubs, he is devoted to a future with Ajax. He is also a member of Denmark's national team and played in the 2018 World Cup.

Position: Forward
Years in Pro Soccer: 2014–Present (Joined Ajax in 2015)
Born: October 6, 1997, Silkeborg, Denmark

Donny van de Beek

Donny van de Beek debuted for the Ajax senior team in 2015 at age 18. By 2017, he was in the regular starting lineup. Van de Beek likes to keep the ball at his feet and has a more offensive than defensive approach to his central midfield position. Although he has scored goals for Ajax, he is more likely to be involved in the play leading to a goal. Van de Beek recently turned down an offer from a larger club, saying he prefers to develop his skills at Ajax. Van de Beek has made five appearances for the Dutch national team.

Position: Midfielder
Years in Pro Soccer: 2015–Present
Born: April 18, 1997, Nijkerkerveen, Netherlands

Matthijs de Ligt

Matthijs de Ligt made his debut for the Ajax senior team just a month after his 17th birthday. He scored a goal from a corner kick in his debut game and became Ajax's second-youngest scorer in team history. De Ligt is considered one of soccer's rising stars because he plays with the skill and versatility of a much more experienced player. De Ligt has already established himself as a team leader and a master defender. He represented the Netherlands in a 2018 World Cup qualifying match against Bulgaria.

Position: Defender
Years in Pro Soccer: 2016–Present (Debuted with Ajax, but also played for the club's reserve team)
Born: August 12, 1999, Leiderdorp, Netherlands

Daley Blind

Daley Blind spent the first six years of his professional career with Ajax before transferring to Manchester United. After four years there, he transferred back to Ajax. He is the son of veteran Ajax player Danny Blind, who spent 13 seasons with the team. Blind has played defensive positions at midfield, left back, and center back. He is known for his tactical awareness and intelligence. Blind has the ability to know when to launch an attack or when to stay back and pass the ball. He has made 58 appearances with the Netherlands national team.

Position: Defender
Years in Pro Soccer: 2008–Present
(2008–2014 and 2018–Present with Ajax)
Born: March 9, 1990, Amsterdam, Netherlands

All-Time Records

16
Youngest Player
At 16, Clarence Seedorf was both the youngest player ever to debut as part of AFC Ajax and the team's youngest player ever to score a goal.

367
Most Goals Scored
Including tournaments and unofficial **friendlies**, Johan Cruyff scored 367 goals during his time as an Ajax forward.

69
Most Games Played Without a Loss
During the 1994–95 season, Ajax played 69 straight league and European matches without a loss.

603

Most Matches Played

Ajax legend Sjaak Swart played in 603 matches for Ajax.

55

Most Goals in a Single Season

Henk Groot scored 55 goals in official matches during the 1960–61 season, a club record.

Timeline

Throughout the team's history, AFC Ajax has had many memorable events that have become defining moments for the team and its fans.

1900
Ajax is founded as an official club.

1956
The Eredivisie, the Netherlands' professional soccer league, is formed with Ajax as a founding member.

1890 1900 1910 1920 1930 1940 1950

In 1915, Jack Reynolds is appointed coach, a move that defines the club's direction for decades.

1934
De Meer Stadion becomes home to AFC Ajax and remains the team's home pitch for more than 60 years.

1995
Legendary coach Louis van Gaal leads Ajax to win the European Champions League, the European Super Cup, and the team's second International Cup.

1972
Johan Cruyff and other legendary players lead Ajax to a National Championship, the Dutch Cup, the European Champions Cup, and the International Cup.

The Future
Although Ajax has enjoyed less success in the past two decades, the team's reputation is still that of a professional soccer powerhouse. With a reputation for producing and developing skilled young players, Ajax has the potential to rise again to the top of the professional soccer world in the coming years.

2014
Ajax wins the Eredivisie title for the fourth straight year, marking the first time in club history that the team has done so.

1960 1970 1980 1990 2000 2010 2020

2018
Amsterdam ArenA is officially renamed Johan Cruyff ArenA in memory of the Ajax legend.

In 1964, Ajax legend Johan Cruyff joins the team.

1996
Amsterdam ArenA becomes AFC Ajax's home stadium.

Write a Biography

Life Story

A person's life story can be the subject of a book. This kind of book is called a biography. Biographies often describe the lives of people who have achieved great success. These people may be alive today, or they may have lived many years ago. Reading a biography can help you learn more about a great person.

Get the Facts

Use research in the library and on the internet to find out more about your favorite soccer player. Learn as much about him or her as you can. What position does he or she play? What are his or her statistics in important categories? Has he or she set any records? Also, be sure to write down key events in the person's life. What was his or her childhood like? What has he or she accomplished off the field? Is there anything else that makes this person special or unusual?

Use the Concept Web

A concept web is a useful research tool. Read the questions in the concept web on the following page. Answer the questions in your notebook. Your answers will help you write a biography.

Concept Web

Write a Biography

Adulthood
- Where does this individual currently reside?
- Does he or she have a family?

Your Opinion
- What did you learn from the books you read in your research?
- Would you suggest these books to others?
- Was anything missing from these books?

Childhood
- Where and when was this person born?
- Describe his or her parents, siblings, and friends.
- Did this person grow up in unusual circumstances?

Accomplishments off the Field
- What is this person's life's work?
- Has he or she received awards or recognition for accomplishments?
- How have this person's accomplishments served others?

Help and Obstacles
- Did this individual have a positive attitude?
- Did he or she receive help from others?
- Did this person have a mentor?
- Did this person face any hardships?
- If so, how were the hardships overcome?

Accomplishments on the Field
- What records does this person hold?
- What key games and plays have defined his or her career?
- What are his or her stats in categories important to his or her position?

Work and Preparation
- What was this person's education?
- What was his or her work experience?
- How does this person work?
- What is the process he or she uses?

Trivia Time

Take this quiz to test your knowledge of AFC Ajax. The answers are printed upside down under each question.

1 What is the name of the top division of Dutch soccer?

A. Eredivisie

2 How long does it take to open or close the roof of Johan Cruyff ArenA?

A. 18 minutes

3 What are AFC Ajax's official colors?

A. Red, black, and white

4 Why is the figure of Ajax on the team's logo drawn with 11 lines?

A. They represent the 11 players on a soccer field.

5 Who is Ajax's longest-serving coach?

A. Jack Reynolds

6 What style of play is Rinus Michels known for introducing during his time at Ajax?

A. Total football

7 Where do Ajax's main ultras groups get their names?

A. From their seating sections

8 Why did Johan Cruyff start wearing the number 14?

A. He won a game after choosing it randomly and then became superstitious about it.

9 Who is the youngest non-Dutch soccer player to score a hat trick for Ajax?

A. Kasper Dolberg

Key Words

clubs: athletic teams or organizations

defenders: also called "backs," players who play in front of the goal and stop the other team from scoring

forwards: players on a soccer team who normally play closest to the opponent's goal and try to score goals

friendlies: matches or games that do not count toward league standings or tournament rankings for a sports team

goalkeepers: also called "goalies," the players responsible for keeping the ball from going into the goal and the only players who are allowed to pick up the ball

hat trick: when a soccer player scores three goals in one game

kit: the standard attire worn by soccer players, including a jersey, shorts, socks, and shin guards

midfielder: a soccer player who plays between the forwards and defenders and can take either a defensive or offensive role

total football: a style of play where outfield players can move into and out of different positions to cover the field

ultras: a type of soccer fans known for extreme support of a club

Index

Log on to www.av2books.com

AV² by Weigl brings you media enhanced books that support active learning. Go to www.av2books.com, and enter the special code found on page 2 of this book. You will gain access to enriched and enhanced content that supplements and complements this book. Content includes video, audio, weblinks, quizzes, a slide show, and activities.

AV² Online Navigation

Audio
Listen to sections of the book read aloud.

Book Pages
AV² pages directly correspond to pages in the book.

Video
Watch informative video clips.

Embedded Weblinks
Gain additional information for research.

Key Words
Study vocabulary, and complete a matching word activity.

Try This!
Complete activities and hands-on experiments.

Quizzes
Test your knowledge.

Slide Show
View images and captions, and prepare a presentation.

AV² was built to bridge the gap between print and digital. We encourage you to tell us what you like and what you want to see in the future.

Sign up to be an AV² Ambassador at www.av2books.com/ambassador.

Due to the dynamic nature of the Internet, some of the URLs and activities provided as part of AV² by Weigl may have changed or ceased to exist. AV² by Weigl accepts no responsibility for any such changes. All media enhanced books are regularly monitored to update addresses and sites in a timely manner. Contact AV² by Weigl at 1-866-649-3445 or av2books@weigl.com with any questions, comments, or feedback.